THE LAMPSHADE KIT

WITH 8 READY-TO-USE LAMPSHADES AND 8 PULL-OUT PATTERNS

AMELIA
ST GEORGE

PHOTOGRAPHS BY
JAN BALDWIN

Trafalgar Square Publishing

NORTH POMFRET, VERMONT

I should like to dedicate this book to some of my
exceptional girl friends, who have been most supportive to me.
Firstly Nana, my mother, my extraordinary daughters
Abigail and Tiphanie and my friends Christine Mengers, Elizabeth
Doumen, Michelle Villemur, Monia Perlhagen,
Nadalette La Fonta, Rosella Spoerry, Susanne Lawson, Sue Frost,
Susan Partridge and last but not least Susan Porjes.

First published in the United States of America in 1994 by
Trafalgar Square Publishing, North Pomfret, Vermont 05053

ISBN: 1-57076-004-7

Editor Cindy Richards
Designer Janet James
Photographer Jan Baldwin

Paper used are natural recyclable products made from wood grown
in sustainable forests.
In addition, the paper in this book is acid free.

Colour Separations by Magnacraft, London
Printed in Hong Kong by Sheck Wah Tong Printing Press Limited

Contents

Introduction

My first attempts at creating lampshades were as a child when I used to make multi-coloured paper lanterns. I adored cutting the slits and diamonds and was charmed to see the fairy lights winking through when they were hung on the tree at Christmas time. Then, as a teenager, for barbecues on the beach, I would fill brown paper bags with a layer of sand and place candles inside – the bags protected the candle flames from the wind. In my garden, when the children were younger, I tied up chicken wire lanterns with candles firmly secured inside away from trailing blankets and little fingers. All these shades, humble though their origins, were decorative, safe and effective.

I hope I have progressed a little in this book, but not too much,

these are all fun ideas aimed to stimulate your imagination so that you too can make your own creations. Lampshade making is straightforward and inexpensive. This book describes the materials you can use and what you will need: it begins with the simplest and easiest shades to create and then, as it progresses, the expertise gained in earlier chapters is reused and built on to achieve the most delicate effects. In addition, there are eight pull-out patterns in the centre of the book, to make things even easier, alongside eight exquisite ready-to-use lampshades which I designed because I should love to have them in my home. All you have to do is cut them out and glue the edges together and you have eight classic little cone shades.

LIGHTING IN THE HOME

Good lighting contributes to the home, adding warmth, excitement, drama or drawing the eye to a treasured corner. At the same time light illuminates, it creates shadows and the stronger and narrower the beam of light the greater the shadow that is created. A large-based coolie lampshade, for example, disperses a large area of light which would be suitable to work by. In contrast, the narrower base of a small conical shade directs the light into an intense pool around the lamp base which would be ideal for lighting *objets d'art* on a small table.

Overhead lighting can sometimes be a problem as although it provides a good overall light source, it produces a dull uniform light with no areas of shadow. This can be adjusted, however, by introducing two or three areas of stronger light to introduce contrast and shadow. There are various methods of using lighting. I have found one of the most versatile and practical for my changing requirements throughout the house, is to use varying sizes of these little classic shaped cones (see page 8). They are quick and easy to make and can be adapted to fit a variety of lamp bases or hanging lights. To decide upon your lighting requirements I suggest you go through your house, room by room, as I have done.

My kitchen has good practical fluorescent lighting hidden under the overhead cupboards which gives me well-lit work surfaces. I resort to overhead lighting for winter breakfasts and tea before the children tackle their home work at the kitchen table. However, for informal family meals all my lamps come into play adorned with a variety of little cone shades. By changing my lighting I can create a particular mood. The warmth of candles filtering light through cut-out lamps (see page 69) transforms a humble family-meal into a small but sumptuous feast.

In my sitting room, I need flexibility. I love open fires so there is always one gently smouldering in my house giving warmth and a wonderful light from the glowing embers. However, as I work from home, I also need a number of good direct light sources positioned all around the room as I tend to move my work about. Even the floor needs illuminating as frequently something or someone is sprawled there. The easiest solution is to introduce lamps both standard and table, all with pivoting shades. Do not be afraid of using different strengths of bulbs around the room: I go from a 25 watt bulb (very subtle) to a bright 100 watt bulb. The ultimate luxury is of course a dimmer switch on the lamp, although these are not always available in Europe.

The girls' room is long and thin with an immensely tall bay window at one end. Unfortunately, I cannot fit a good large table in the window recess so the table is situated half-way down the room. It is crucial to have a good light source here so that the children are not in shadow while working. I have therefore placed two table lamps here to provide adequate lighting. For my older children, bedside lamps are essential to avoid quarrels over late night reading. The shades can be pivoted and by using a dark opaque shade the light can be tilted away from the sleeping sister and onto the chapter in question. For very young children, safety must always come first. A hanging light or a table lamp with a low watt bulb are the best choices. Make sure you tape any trailing flexes to the back of solid furniture and cover any additional electric sockets with socket covers.

The dining room is either a hive of activity or a quiet retreat. For a civilized dinner, I use straight-sided candles coupled with pretty shades thus avoiding trailing flexes from the table. Opaque shades lined with metallic or gold paper work particularly well as the light is reflected to form a pool of light at the base of the candle holders which is most flattering on the laugh lines and is conducive to conversation because no one is in the spotlight. If you need a little more light to dine by while still retaining a gentle feel to the evening I recommend the cut trellis stencil (see page 69). It is sensational when lit, casting flickering shadows over the ceiling to create the most intriguing ambience.

For busy lunches the more translucent shades, the little white silhouette lamps (see page 86) or the cherubs (see page 85), give a warm and dispersed light, also lovely for summer dinners. Or for a chatty lunch with girl friends, may be with children dashing in and out, the flower and butterfly shade (see page 65) adds a civilizing influence.

In my tiny bedroom, the lighting must be adaptable for the early morning rush, especially in the winter, or for an early night, snuggling into bed with bedtime stories, or now more frequently my older children's views on the Classics. So the lighting must be kind but good. My bedside table is relatively small so I have cheated with three lamps on one base. This looks luxurious while being practical. A larger lamp on my chest of drawers gives more light for dark mornings.

Do not forget the hall and corridors, a narrow table or shelf by the door will take a lamp with a few welcoming flowers and will be a kind introduction to your home. Used with a timing switch it could also act as a deterrent to burglars.

Special safety regulations apply, of course, to bathrooms and there should be no electric sockets in this room – unless it is a special one for an electric razor.

Lamps and their shades should enable you to vary the lighting in your home with precision and without upsetting the balance and harmony of a room – so use them. If, like me, you tend to change details for special events, seasons and people then this book will be your dream. Making lampshades is not a difficult skill to master and enables you to have instant decorations to suit every occasion. The classic little cones do not even need frames to support them just the metal fitting shown on page 17. This means you can clip them together with paper clips when they are in use and store them flat when not. Experiment and have fun.

Amelia Saint George

THE
READY-TO-USE
LAMPSHADES

You will find these eight ready-to-use lampshades in the
centre of the book. They have been designed to fit over most small
lamp bases using the attachment shown on page 17.
To assemble, cut around the outline of the shade with a cutting knife
or pair of scissors. Spread some all-purpose glue along
the overlap edge indicated by the dotted line (see below). Join the
two edges together and hold in place with
paper-clips until the glue is dry – nothing could be easier.

NOTE The ready-to-use lampshades and the tracing paper
patterns can be removed from the book by prising apart
the single staple in the centre and lifting these pages out.

*From left to right: Farmyard; Sun and Moon (top row); Green and White Stripes; Willow
Pattern; Cherubs (centre row); Découpage Flowers; Blue and White Stripes; Holly and Mistletoe*

CHAPTER ONE

BEGINNINGS

Lampshades come in a great variety of shapes and sizes: cones, squares, drums, straight and scalloped edged, large and small. Despite the diversity it is possible to use the same basic method to make a lampshade whatever its shape. All you need is a metal lampshade frame in the shape of your choice which you can buy from specialist shops or, if you wish to revamp an existing shade, you can just strip off the old covering. Then, following the simple step-by-step instructions below, you can make your pattern to suit your frame. Once you have done this you are ready to start making your own shades in whatever colour, pattern or design you wish.

MAKING A BASIC LAMPSHADE PATTERN

It is very difficult to envisage the shape of pattern you will need for certain lampshade shapes. The photograph opposite illustrates the range of metal frames available and beneath each their paper pattern. You may be surprised how large some of them are and if, like me, you do not have a very big table then you can always draw around your shade on the floor.

You can use the same basic method to make a pattern for a lampshade frame whatever its size or shape.

WHAT YOU WILL NEED

Lampshade frame of your choice

Roll of lining paper

Pencil

Ruler

Scissors

1 Take your frame and place it on its side. Roll it across the lining paper and trace the path of the top and bottom of the frame with a pencil as I am doing in the photograph opposite. Make a little felt-tip mark or stick a piece of tape at the point of the frame where you plan to start so that you know when you have traced round the whole circumference. Allow a 1cm ($^3/_8$in) overlap.

2 Remove the shade and you will be left with two pencil lines marking the top and base of the shade. Join them together at either end using a ruler and cut around the pencil lines. Check the pattern fits the frame by joining the ends with paper clips and placing it over the frame.

3 Attach the paper pattern to the paper or fabric of your choice (see page 12 for information about suitable materials) and cut around the pattern.

Finish off your shade by following the instructions on page 13.

CHOOSING PAPERS AND MATERIALS

You can use practically any type of paper or fabric to make a lampshade so long as you
follow certain safety guidelines (see page 16). An old newspaper, a colourful page from a magazine,
tissue paper, wrapping paper, wallpaper, silks, hessian – the list is endless – all make
suitable coverings. There are also some wonderful handmade papers available which make the
most exquisite shades as can be seen from the lampshade shown on the cover of this book.

The only point you have to remember is that if you are making a shade for a large frame then you will probably have to back it (see page 14) to give it added strength. On the other hand if you are making one of the classic cone shapes that we give patterns for throughout the book then you don't even need a frame, as a 5cm (2in) diameter, 16.5cm (6½in) height metal support will be sufficient (see Fittings and Fixtures, page 17).

It is probably a good idea to experiment with a smaller shade first as they are so quick and easy to make.

It is also worth holding up any paper or fabric you plan to use against a light source so that you can see what effect it will give. If you do this with several contrasting papers you will become aware of how the light that is cast is affected by the colour and pattern of the paper. Reds, oranges and yellows give a warm glow while blues and greens give a cool hard light. Dark brown, navy, burgundy and black create a dramatic atmosphere but do not allow much light through and so would not, for example, be a good choice if you wished to make a shade for a reading light.

Patterned materials tend to soften the light, as do textured fabrics and papers. Silk looks soft during the day, and when lit the natural slub is exaggerated and adds an interesting texture to the shade which is an added delight.

Metallic papers reflect back light and therefore when made into a shade create an interesting pool of light around the lamp base.

These striking lampshades were made from
wallpaper (front) and fabric (behind).
They were both lined (see page 14) to give
the finished shades added strength.

HOW TO LINE
PAPER AND FABRIC SHADES

Don't be put off using a certain type of paper because you think it is too flimsy
as you can always line it using another thicker paper or even with a special plastic sheeting (available
from picture framers). The latter is particularly good for backing fabrics (see below).

Leftover wallpaper or fabric lengths are an ideal and practical choice of covering for a lampshade. They immediately give a co-ordinated effect to a room and are a good way of making use of excess paper and fabric trimmings. You may find, however, that you need to line your wallpaper or fabric shades to give them added strength. This is very simple to do and is worth the extra effort to give your shade a really professional finish.

1 Paper Make a pattern for your shade (see page 10) and use it to cut out the shade from the wallpaper length or covering of your choice. Lay the backing paper on the table. Apply some glue to the back of the cut-out shade and stick it on to the backing paper. Allow to dry and cut around the shade outline as shown. It is as simple as that!

2 Fabric For smaller shades you can use interfacing (see page 89) but for larger shades like this, I strongly recommend using a plastic backing as it is quick to use and does not discolour. Fold back the edges of your fabric and tack into place. Gradually peel off the protective covering from the plastic sheeting and smooth your fabric on to the adhesive layer beneath. Then cut around the outline of the fabric. Remove any tacking stitches.

3 Attaching to the frame Glue the edges together on both the wallpaper and fabric shades as shown on page 9. Hold in place until dry using large paper clips. Apply a light non-coloured glue to the top and base rims of your metal frame. Invert the shade and place the frame inside. Press into position and leave to dry. It is not necessary to glue small shades into position as they sit quite happily on the frames.

WHAT YOU WILL NEED

Wallpaper

Fabric

Backing paper
(I used lining paper for the wallpaper shade and plastic sheeting for the fabric shade)

Scissors

Spray glue or any suitable all-purpose glue

Pencil case contents

FINISHING OFF

It is quite a good idea to cover your finished shades with some sort of protective surface particularly if they are large. Fixative is good for paper shades while many fabric sprays are not only ideal for protecting fabrics but can also be used on paper. Take care when you use these sprays to follow the instructions on the can carefully and use them in a well-ventilated room.

I have tried to varnish paper lamps to make them more durable, but with very mixed results. Oil based varnish discolours the paper, and clear acrylic varnish warps it badly. However I have had good results with spray varnish which is available from hardware shops.

I suggest, however, that you approach varnishing with caution, and always try some out on a piece of scrap paper before attempting to coat a shade you have just made. This procedure may seem laborious but at least it avoids any disasters; you don't want to spend ages making a pretty lampshade only to find the varnish discolours or warps it.

Another way of sealing and protecting paper shades is to cover them with a solution of diluted PVA glue. The solution is white, but don't be alarmed as it becomes transparent when dry.

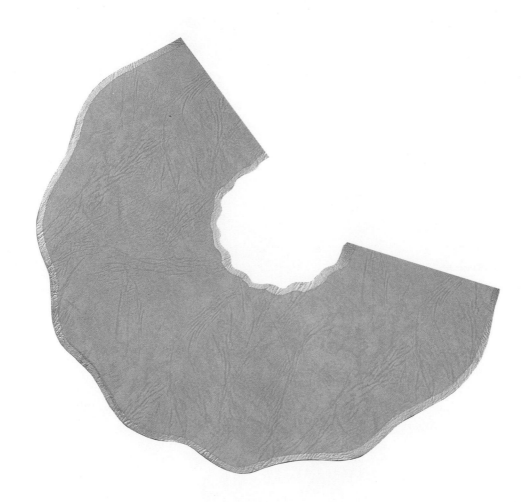

BULBS AND LIGHTING

Bulbs come in a variety of sizes, shapes and strengths as can be seen from the photograph below. The ones most commonly used are 40, 60 and 100 watt bulbs. A 100 watt bulb would be a suitable light for a pendant light while a 40 or 60 watt bulb would be good for a desk or reading light. At the other end of the scale a 7 watt bulb gives very little light but is ideal for use as a child's night light.

When you put a shade over a light bulb, you always lessen the bulb's brightness. In addition, a shade helps to direct the light which is very useful if you wish to light a specific area. The photograph of the silhouette lamps (see page 86) illustrates how shades can affect the light source. Each of the silhouette lamps is fitted with a 15 watt bulb. The red shade lined with black is totally opaque so the light is dispersed as a wide pool at the base of the shade. This would be an ideal light for illuminating a small *objet d'art* beneath it but no more. The small silhouette lamp gives a soft, subtle light and would be an ideal light to dine by. The larger cream shade again gives a soft subtle light and with a 40 watt bulb would make a comfortable reading lamp. The red lamp, however, would never be appropriate for such a purpose.

Bulbs come in a great variety of shapes and sizes: from large bulbous ones suitable for a pendant light to small ones ideal for use with delicate little shades.

SAFETY
You should always follow proper fire safety precautions and make sure you do not have your bulb too close to the paper shade. There should be a minimum clearance of 3cm (1¼in) between a 40 watt bulb and one of the small classic cone shaped shades shown throughout the book. A 40 watt bulb is the maximum wattage that we recommend using with these small paper shades. Never exceed the maximum wattage stated on the fitting.

There must be no electric plug sockets in bathrooms and all light fittings must be completely enclosed and all switches must be pull cords.

Fire brigade regulations only cover emergency exit lighting, so do be cautious and make sure that you will not be needing their assistance.

FITTINGS AND FIXTURES

Fittings and fixtures vary dramatically between countries as do voltages so check your particular requirements with a local supplier. However the fixtures and fittings shown below are available throughout the world.

Bulb clip: this small metal attachment is very adaptable and fits over both narrow and wide bulbs. It is ideal for using under small light shades (**1**).

Candle followers: these are quite delightful, but they must always be used with straight-sided candles and not left unsupervised. For dining in the evening or a winter lunch they add refinement and intimacy (**2**).

Shade holders: these alter the height between lamp base and shade and can be adjusted to fit the requirements of your lamp. You can buy plastic and metal ones: the little brass holders shown here are just the right size for the classic little cone shades featured throughout the book and for the ready-to-use lampshades. Smaller bought lampshades often have the

shade holders incorporated into the metal shade (**3**).

Pendant light fittings: hanging from the ceiling these can look fun with huge global bulbs and a coolie shade. You can incorporate dimmers and timed lighting bayonets into the fitting of your lamp. These are very practical and I have used a dimmer by my bed and a timed light in the children's room (**4**).

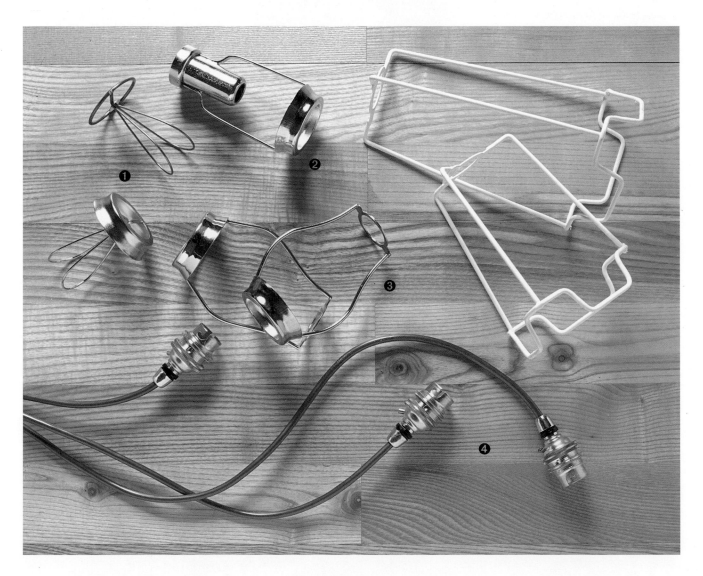

CHAPTER TWO

THE PULL-OUT PATTERNS

Many people find the thought of designing something from scratch rather daunting, but in this book you will have no such problems as there are eight ready-to-use tracing paper patterns in the centre of the book (see pages 41-55). Simply decide which background paper you would like and then trace off the design following the step-by-step instructions given below.

I rather liked colouring by numbers as a child and always remember the excitement as gradually some great master was revealed. In the same way I thought it would be fun to play with the colour and background papers on these little shades to see what masters I could create. Throughout the book I have used the tracings, or elements from them, so that you can see for yourselves the variety of effects that can be achieved using different papers and colours.

WHAT YOU WILL NEED

Pull-out patterns
(pages 41-55)

Scissors

Soft pencil (2B)

Background paper (see page 12 for
list of suitable papers)

Tracing paper (optional)

1 Select a pattern you like and cut out the whole page rather than just cutting around the lampshade shape. I decided to use the fleur-de-lys pattern on page 43. Using a soft pencil, go over the outline of the whole design. Then place the tracing, pencil-side down, on to your chosen paper (or fabric) attaching it to the paper with a little adhesive or masking tape to avoid movement. Trace over the outline again, but quite firmly this time, so that the pencil markings underneath are transferred to the background paper.

2 If you have chosen to trace on to a dark background paper, such as a burgundy or bottle green, the pencil markings may not show. If this is the case outline the tracing with a yellow or white coloured crayon instead of a pencil. Attach the tracing to your paper as before and go over the outline firmly with pencil so that the coloured markings are transferred to your paper. Remove the tracing paper and, should you need to, redefine the outline using the coloured pencil.

NOTE If you do not wish to cut the tracing out of the book then simply trace the design on to a piece of tracing paper and follow the method above to transfer it to your chosen background paper.

USING A PHOTOCOPIER

Another way of using the traced patterns in this book, or any of the other designs shown, is by using a photocopier. You may be lucky enough to have access to one at work but if not many libraries and newsagents now have them. It costs very little to photocopy and it is worth trying this method as it gives you so much freedom and variety. For your background, you can choose from the wide range of delightful wrapping papers available.

The great advantage of using a photocopier is the speed and ease with which you can transfer designs to your background papers. It is especially useful if the design you wish to use has intricate details which would be tricky to transfer using the tracing method. For example, I simply photocopied the little cherub motifs from page 57 to use on the lampshade shown on page 85. To have traced off this design would have taken quite some time and the result would not have been as good.

The drawback of using a photocopier is that you are limited by the size of paper the photocopier will take. If you wish to make a large shade you will need to use the tracing method. I photocopied the fleur-de-lys design on to a variety of backgrounds (see page 22 for the results) but you can use any of the patterns in just the same way, simply follow the instructions on the right.

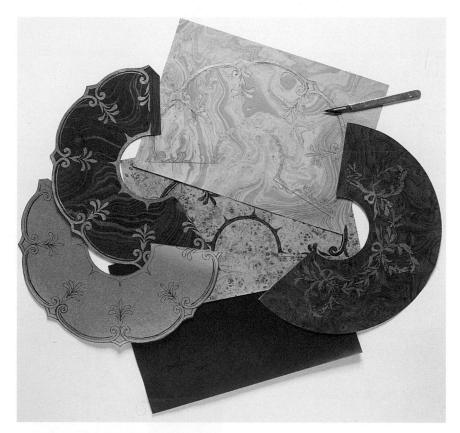

This colourful selection of shades was made by photocopying the fleur-de-lys, classic and roman ornament designs (see pages 43-47) on to a variety of different background papers.

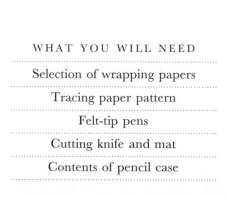

WHAT YOU WILL NEED

Selection of wrapping papers

Tracing paper pattern

Felt-tip pens

Cutting knife and mat

Contents of pencil case

1 Cut your wrapping paper down to the same size as the photocopier paper and place right side down in the paper tray. Next, place your tracing paper pattern on to the photocopying glass and copy in the normal way.

2 Your tracing paper design will appear as a black outline on your background paper. You can then use felt-tip pens or other materials to fill in or outline the design. For more information on colouring in see pages 20-23. I find felt-tips are particularly good for colouring over dark backgrounds.

3 Once you are happy with your design, cut around the outline edge of the shade and glue the edges together (see page 9).

NOTE Do check the weight of paper that your photocopier will tolerate, most photocopiers take up to 130gms (60lbs). If it is too thick (or too thin) the copier will jam.

COLOURING IN BACKGROUNDS

When decorating it is usual to pick a colour scheme for each room. I find the drawback
with this approach is that I have all sorts of bits and pieces that need accommodating but which don't go
with my required ideal. I get around this by re-covering a chair in a toning fabric, changing
the cushions or by playing with the paints on the walls so that gradually my oddments fit in.

TARTAN SHADE

This traditional pattern is incredibly versatile because of the unexpected wealth of colours hidden within the design which can blend into both classic or contemporary interiors. Use the tartan pattern from the centre of the book or use your own family tartan, if you have one, or like me invent one. You can then colour it in using crayons, watercolours, gouache paints, acrylics or felt-tips pens. All give a slightly different effect as can be seen from the photographs below. Choose the one you like and have a go: you could even combine watercolours with crayons for added variety.

WHAT YOU WILL NEED

Tartan pattern (page 41)

Rough paper for experimenting

A4 paper of your choice (use cartridge paper for coloured pencils and felt-tips, watercolour paper for watercolours, acrylics and gouache)

Crayons, felt-tip pens, watercolours, acrylics and gouache

Brushes

Pencil case contents

1 Transfer the tartan outline on to a piece of rough paper using the tracing method (see page 18).

2 Colour in the descending parallels first, then the circular parallels. As the colours cross a delightful new hue will appear. The more you cross the lines the greater the variety of colours.

3 Experiment with a number of different media until you find the one you are happy with. Then, retrace the outline on to your chosen background paper and colour as before.

4 Cut out the lampshade and glue the edges together (see page 9). If you want to make more than one shade, simply repeat the process.

Coloured Pencils

Coloured pencils are easy to use and give a delicate effect, just colour each parallel and then use the same colours on the circular lines and watch the different colours appear. Use a ruler when marking in the descending lines to ensure they are straight.

Watercolours

When using watercolours or acrylics, start by choosing three colours. I used ultramarine, crimson alizarin and cadmium yellow – the three primaries whose boldness I love. Make a pool of each colour on your palette and load your brush well. Start by filling in a couple of the descending parallels and then one or two of the circular parallels. Repeat using the other colours. Watercolours give a wonderful impressionistic effect as the colours blend and run depending on how wet they are. I was very critical of my first strokes but was pleasantly surprised with the end result. This shade looks quite beautiful when lit (see opposite), so do not be worried by the odd wobble in your brush stroke.

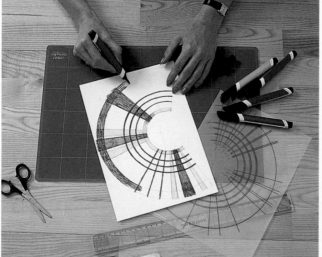

Felt-Tip Pens

Felt-tip pens are more dramatic. I raided my children's box of crayons for these. The ones that were just about to run out gave a grainy effect that looks like the texture of linen while the newer ones were very bold. They looked rather good traversing one another, so have a go.

NOTE It is easier to colour the shades when they are flat. Once you have decorated your shade, allow it to dry and then cut around the outline edge.

FLEUR-DE-LYS SHADE

I am particularly fond of this ancient heraldic lily which
looks wonderful superimposed on a range of different backgrounds.
You can use the same method for all of the traced patterns,
so it is up to you to keep a good look out for interesting background
papers. Play with ideas – what about the pink Financial Times
with a smart fleur-de-lys design photocopied on to it.

I have used a range of plain back-grounds for my fleurs-de-lys shades and it is amazing the different effect created by each. For sophistication try black and gold fleurs-de-lys on a white background or for something more traditional silver on royal blue. The choice is yours.

Look upon these lamps as little decorative details that can be changed depending upon the mood you wish to create. They are inexpensive and easy to make so why not make a pile of them? You can store them flat and when needed simply fasten them together with paper clips rather than using glue.

1 Trace or photocopy the fleur-de-lys design on to your chosen background.

2 You can then either go over the traced outline of the fleurs-de-lys in a colour of your choice or block in the whole shape with colour. Obviously the effectiveness of this depends on the colour and pattern of the background. I find that black and metallic gold and silver felt-tips give the best results over dark backgrounds.

3 Cut out the shade and join the edges together with glue (see page 9). If you have used a very flimsy paper then you will need to back your lampshade with some lining paper (see page 14) before you cut it out.

I created the lampshades shown here using the following backgrounds and outline colours:

Silver and blue shade

I used an embossed ultramarine blue paper and blocked in the fleurs-de-lys motifs using a metallic silver felt-tip.

Black and gold shades

I photocopied the fleur-de-lys pattern on to plain white backgrounds and filled in the motifs using black and gold felt tips.

Large silver shade

I photocopied the fleurs-de-lys pattern onto a large piece of white parchment (A3 size). I then enlarged the original pattern on the photocopier by 100 per cent and transferred a row of the enlarged fleurs-de-lys to the base of the shade using the tracing method and blocked them in with a silver felt-tip.

WHAT YOU WILL NEED

Fleur-de-lys pattern (page 43)

Background papers

Black, gold and silver felt-tip pens

Pencil case contents

CLASSIC SHADE

I adore the elegance of this scroll design and have used these shades again and again
as table decorations. Again do experiment with differing backgrounds using the photocopier.

Pick out a colour from your background paper for filling in the scroll design to give a more natural feel to your work. For example, the red marbled paper I used here has a trace of gold running through it so I filled in the scroll design with a metallic gold felt-tip for a soft and intriguing effect. I also used black felt-tip pens to give a bolder look (see below).

WHAT YOU WILL NEED

Classic pattern (page 45)

Roman ornament pattern (page 47)

Background papers

Black and metallic silver and gold felt-tip pens

Cutting mat and knife

Pencil case contents

1 Photocopy (or trace) the classic design on to your chosen background paper.

2 Block in the scroll design using felt-tip pens. For a slightly three-dimensional effect add a few accents with a black felt tip alongside the gold outlines. The effect is stunning.

3 Cut out and glue the edges together as before. Take care when cutting around the classic edge as it is quite fiddly (see page 27 for further advice).

NOTE

The classic tracing also makes a perfect embroidery pattern for
satin stitch, just follow the steps for the Initial Shade on page 88.

ROMAN ORNAMENT SHADE

Rich in movement, the tracing for this design can be found on page 47. As before, I simply photocopied the traced pattern on to a selection of papers including a sage-green one, and brown, and red marbled papers. Take care, however, when choosing papers as when I first started making shades I made several mistakes. On finding the right colour paper I would use it only to find that when lit it had an underlying texture running though it. I now check every paper before I use it to see what hidden textures there may be and I suggest you do the same – some will look lovely but others can ruin the effect.

Both the classic shades (right) and the roman ornament shades (left) make enchanting table decorations.

CHAPTER THREE

CREATING EDGES

Edges are fun and there are so many different ways of using them. You can create a variety of effects by cutting simple shapes around the top and base edges of your shade, for example, add movement and softness with the smooth wavy scallops (see page 49 for pattern) or for a young girl's bedroom try the pretty trailing flower and butterfly border (see page 53) or for something more contemporary, bold geometric cuts may be just the thing. Edge them with colour using crayons, paints, felt-tips, or trim with braids, beads, raffia or ribbons. A glance through this book will reveal what can be achieved with the greatest of ease.

SIMPLE CUT EDGES

There are a number of ready-to-use patterns in the centre of the book to enable you to make your own cut edge borders. All you need to do is trace off the pattern of your choice on to your paper as shown on page 18. You can either leave the edge as it is or embellish it further using some of the ideas given below.

It is important to cut out these edges accurately for the best effect. A sharp cutting knife or a good pair of scissors is an essential tool. For safety reasons, remember to cut away from your hand if using a knife.

NOTE Do remember that you can enlarge any of the tracings on a photocopier if you wish to make a larger shade.

These elegant scalloped-edged shades were cut from a textured watercolour paper. For added colour, I punched a few holes in one of the shades and threaded through some ribbon.

Wavy Scallops

The elegant undulating curves of this edge (see page 49 for pattern) give a soft flowing movement to the finished shade. Whether cut from a textured watercolour paper (see opposite) or from an embossed black paper lined with gold foil and edged with a trailing black bead fringe, the wavy scallop edge looks exceptional.

Scooped Scallops

These tight scooped scallops (see page 51 for pattern) are both traditional when used on darker papers and quite contemporary when used with brighter hues. This edge looks magical when pierced, you do need a little practice though, detailed instructions are on page 73.

Classic Edge

This edge is part of the classic shade (see page 45 for pattern) but do use it as an edge, it is so pretty. For an alternative treatment try gluing some fine cording around it to give even greater definition. Just by changing the texture and weight of the paper, the shade looks different, so do experiment.

Flower and Butterfly Edge

Adapt designs from other parts of the book to use as decorative edges such as this trailing flower and butterfly edge which is an adaptation of the flower and butterfly stencil (see page 53). This pretty gentle edge is ideal for thicker braids, dangling tassels and gathered ribbons. There are so many tempting possibilities.

ATTACHING BRAID, BEADS AND FRINGES

If you want something slightly more ornate than a simple cut edge then why not
decorate your shade with a luxurious length of braid, an exotic beaded trim or an elegant fringe?
Such decorative edges are easy to achieve as long as you are careful to choose the right
thickness of braid or fringe to suit your shade's requirements. Too thick a braid, for example, will
weigh down a small delicate shade and distort the shape.

1 Measure the edge you wish to decorate by laying the trim around the edge of the shade. Don't forget the top of the shade which looks good edged too. Add a couple of centimetres (about one inch) to your final measurement to allow for fraying.

When measuring the braid for the scalloped edges do remember to measure each one patiently and multiply by the number of scallops around the edge.

2 If you are making a paper lampshade from scratch then attach the trim to the shade before you glue the ends together so that you can lay it flat on the table. If you are using a glue gun, squeeze out about 4cm (3½ in) at a time, glue down the trim and repeat as it dries so quickly. When using conventional transparent hobby glue, apply a little glue to the whole edge and then press down the trim.

3 Leave the shades flat until the glue has completely dried. Don't be tempted, as I am always, to pick them up too soon as the braids will droop down. When dry glue the edges together (see page 9).

4 If you are attaching a trim to a fabric shade, I recommend you stitch it to the shade edge. Do not work with your shade flat as it will buckle when curved into its final form. Pin the shade into shape and lightly stitch the braid on to the edge in the most discreet way possible. Try to avoid gluing as this discolours as it ages.

VARIATIONS

Try using a length of a favourite-coloured ribbon as a decorative edge. Measure it out in the same way as described above. Alternatively, you could make your own multi-coloured tasselled fringe from oddments of leftover wool. This would look delightful in a child's bedroom.

DECORATIVE EDGES

There are so many possible trimmings you could use to edge your shades that it would be impossible to list them all. Go to a specialist shop or the haberdashery department of a large department store and see what is available. Collect a few samples if you can and with these tucked in an envelope, decide on the papers or fabrics for your shade. Having said all that, one of my favourite shades is made from an old envelope with a simple raffia trim. It was an inspirational combination that just worked and that I made while I was carefully planning my next project.

The simple addition of a length of upholstery braid, border of trailing beads or luxuriant fringe, gives your lampshade that special finishing touch.

The collection of lampshades overleaf illustrates the range of possibilities: the shade on the left is edged with a piece of upholstery braid and the red shade behind with an exotic trim of black trailing beads. The rich rosebud needlepoint shade has a thick co-ordinating fringe while the more delicate cross-stich shade (far right) is trimmed with a burgundy cord. The translucent musical shade has touches of gold as a highlight in the black woven braid. The red silhouette lamp is made from two layers of paper; a thick black paper backs a lighter embossed red wrapping paper. The red paper is cut slightly smaller than the black leaving a skirt of black around both the top and base of the shade.

OVERLEAF *(from left to right): Kew Garden print shade with green braid, red shade with trailing bead trim, rosebud needlepoint shade, musical shade with black and gold braid, silhouette shade edged with black paper, and rosebud cross-stitch shade with burgundy cord.*

COLOURING EDGES

You can create a number of different borders by painting bands of colour around both
the top and base edges of the shade. It is a very quick and inexpensive way of embellishing a shade.
I used black and silver felt-tip pens to decorate the edges shown here but you can use
crayons or paints to equal effect.

WHAT YOU WILL NEED

Cutout shade shape
of your choice

Felt-tip pens, paints,
or crayons

1 Cut out your shade from your
chosen background paper. I used some
parchment for my shade and the wavy
scalloped edge tracing from page 49.

2 Lay your shade flat on the table and
edge both top and bottom with a thick
black felt-tip pen (or colour of your
choice). Finally, glue the edges
together and it is ready for use.

VARIATIONS

Try creating a zig-zag edge effect – this could look fun on
a lampshade for a children's room or an alphabetical
border is another possibility.

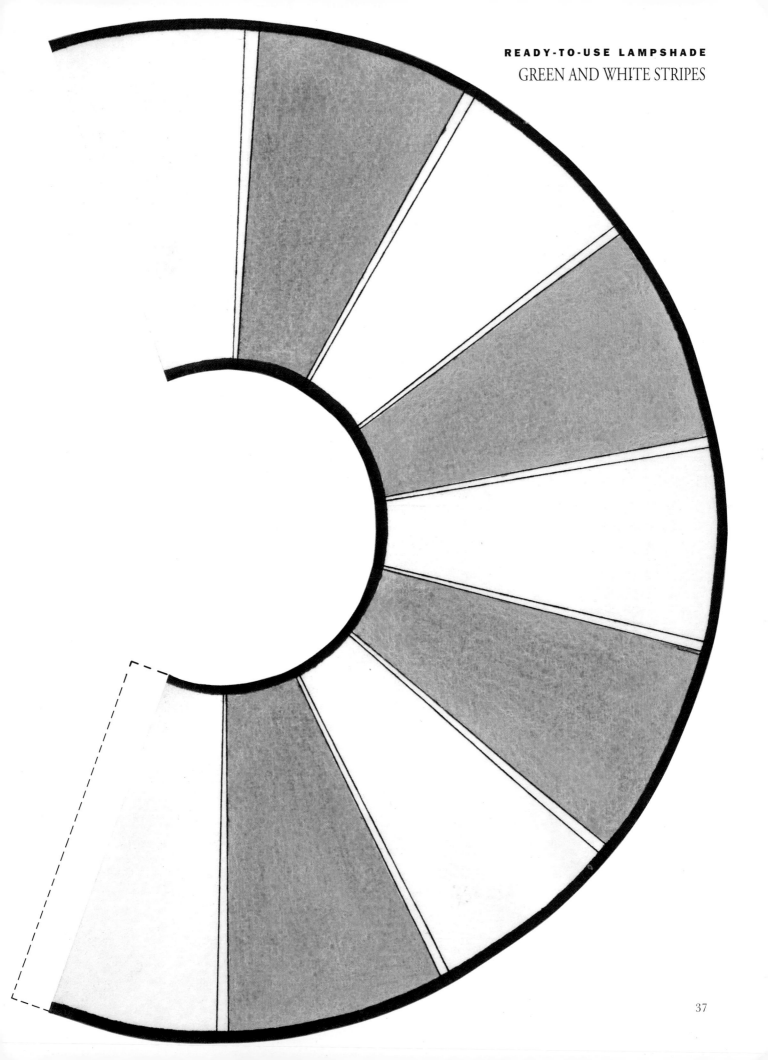

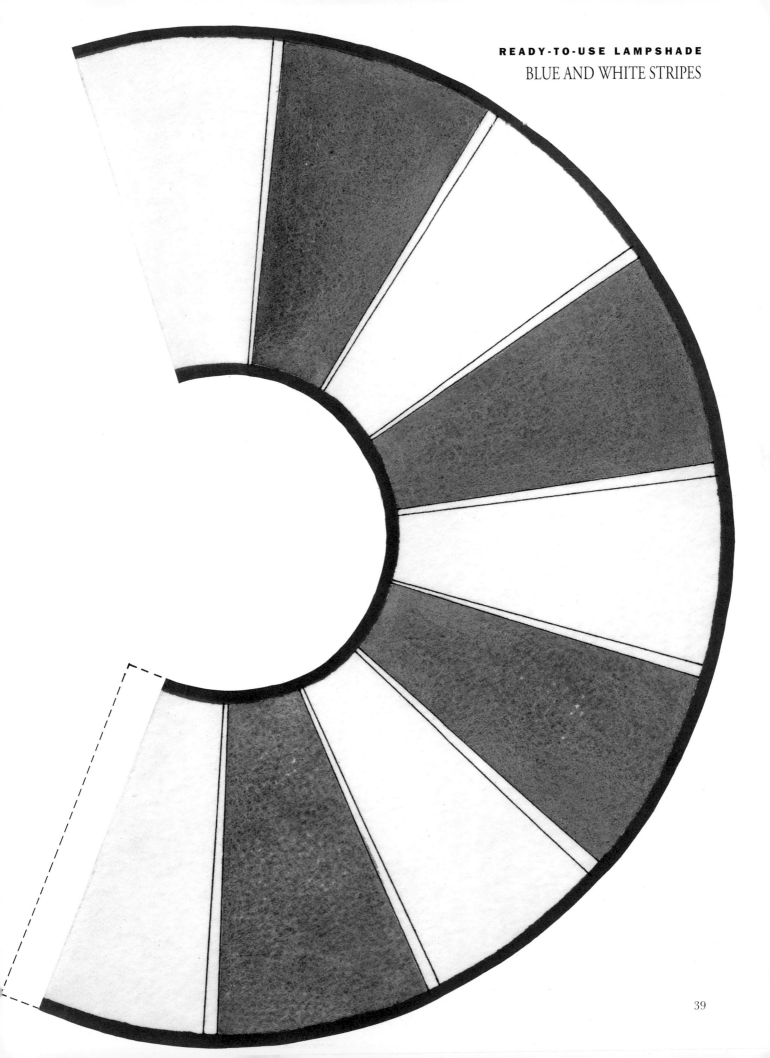

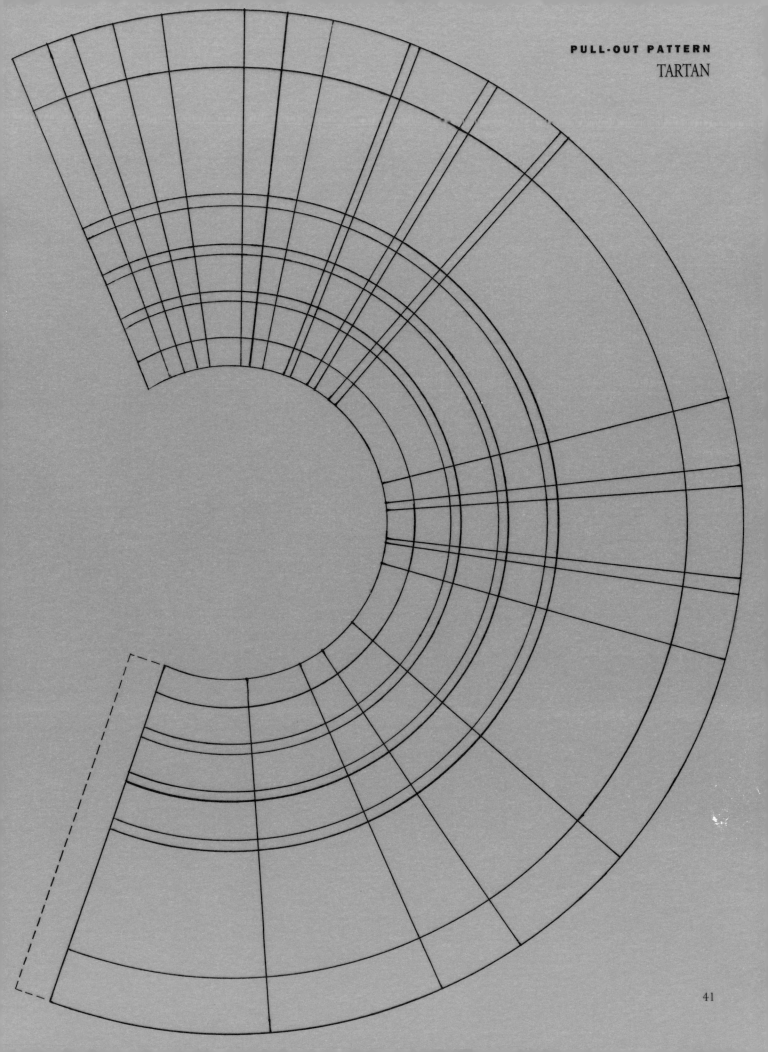

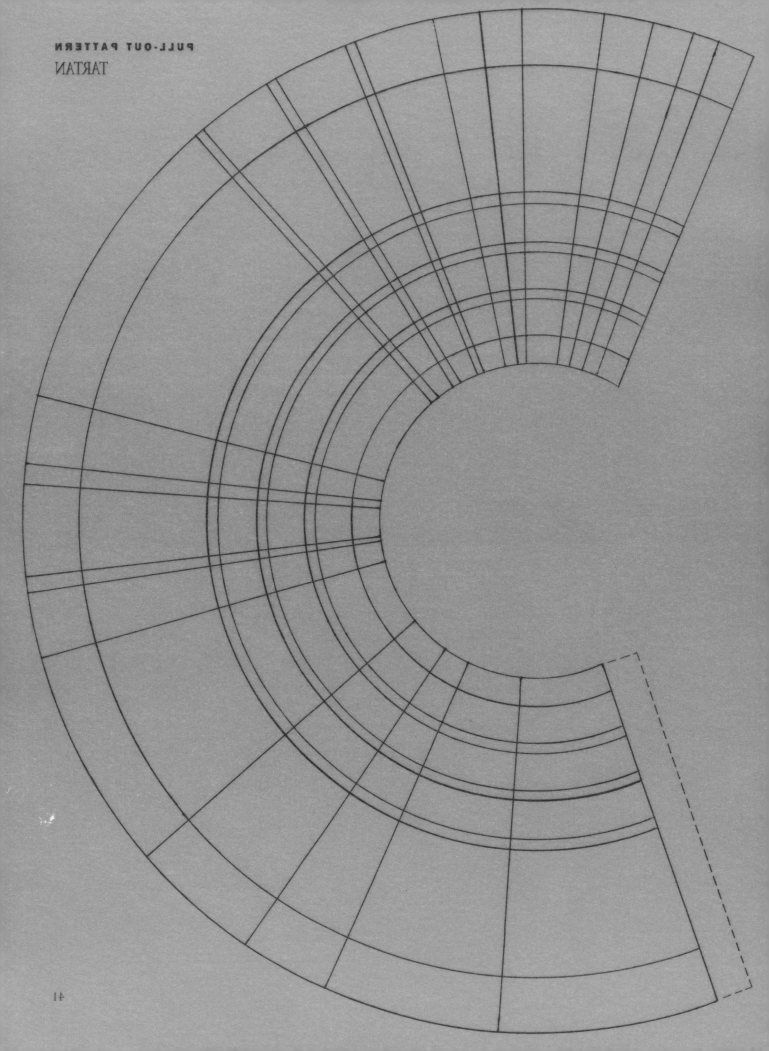

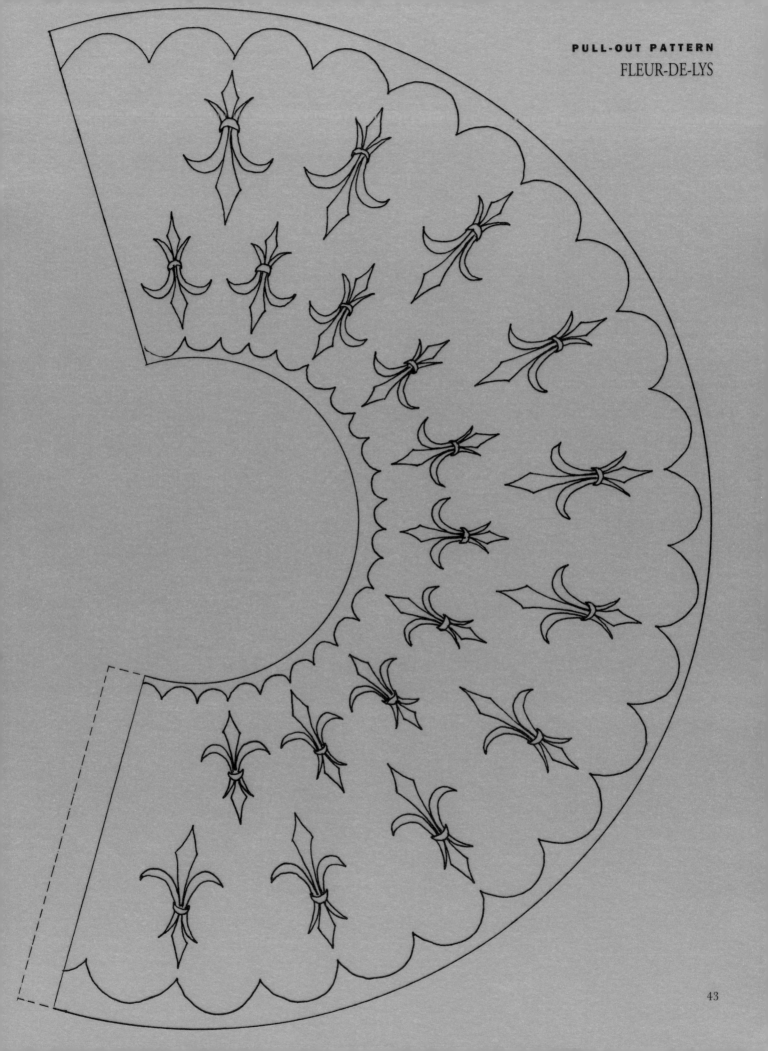

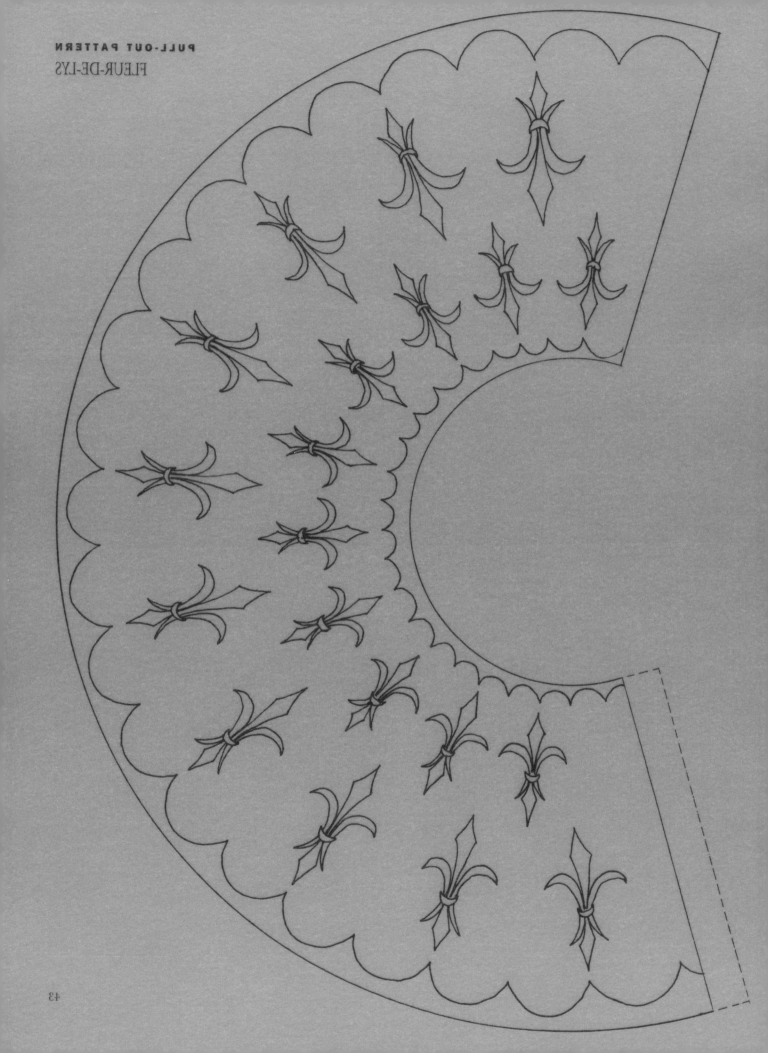

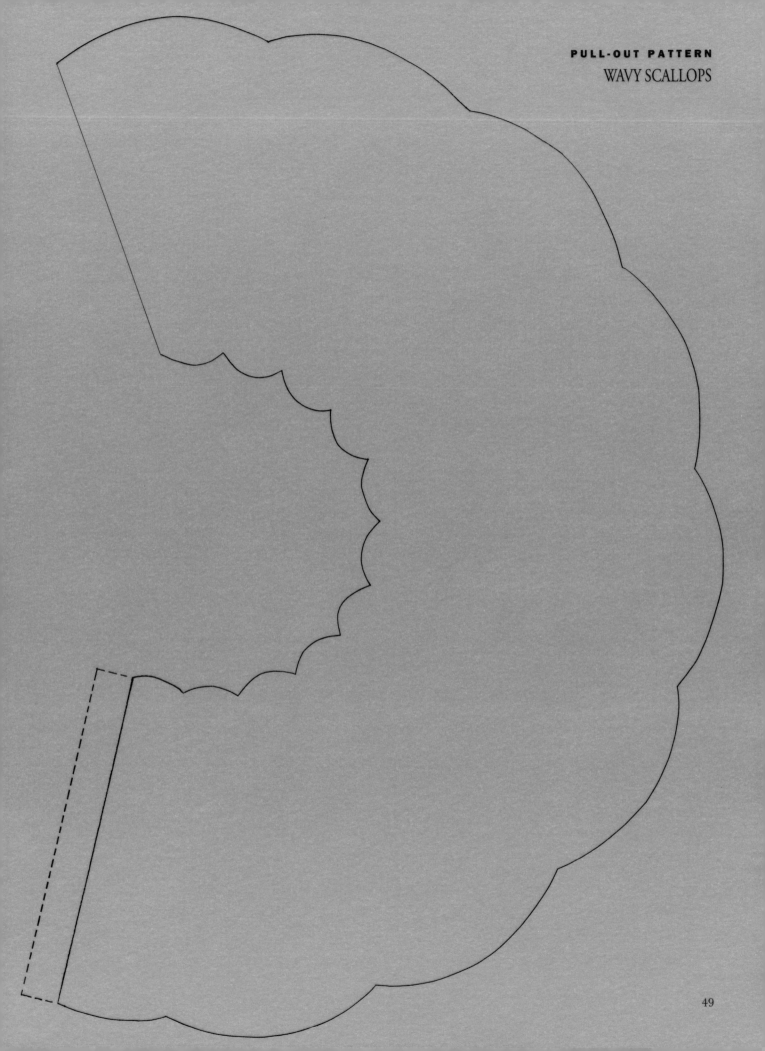

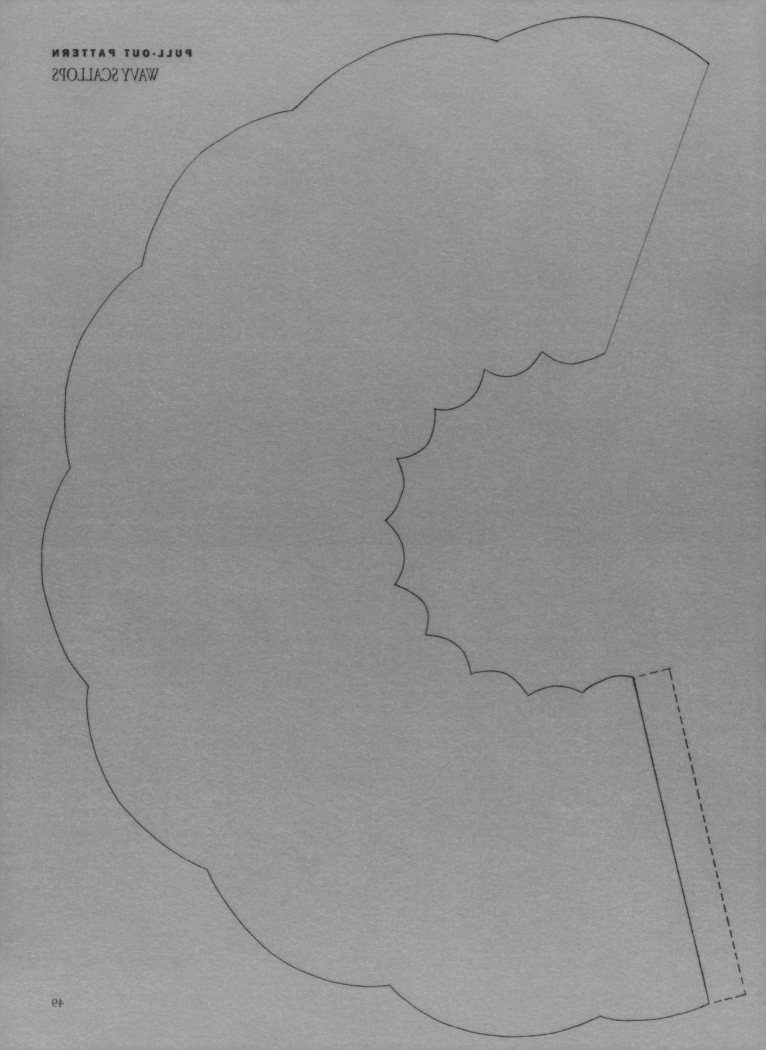

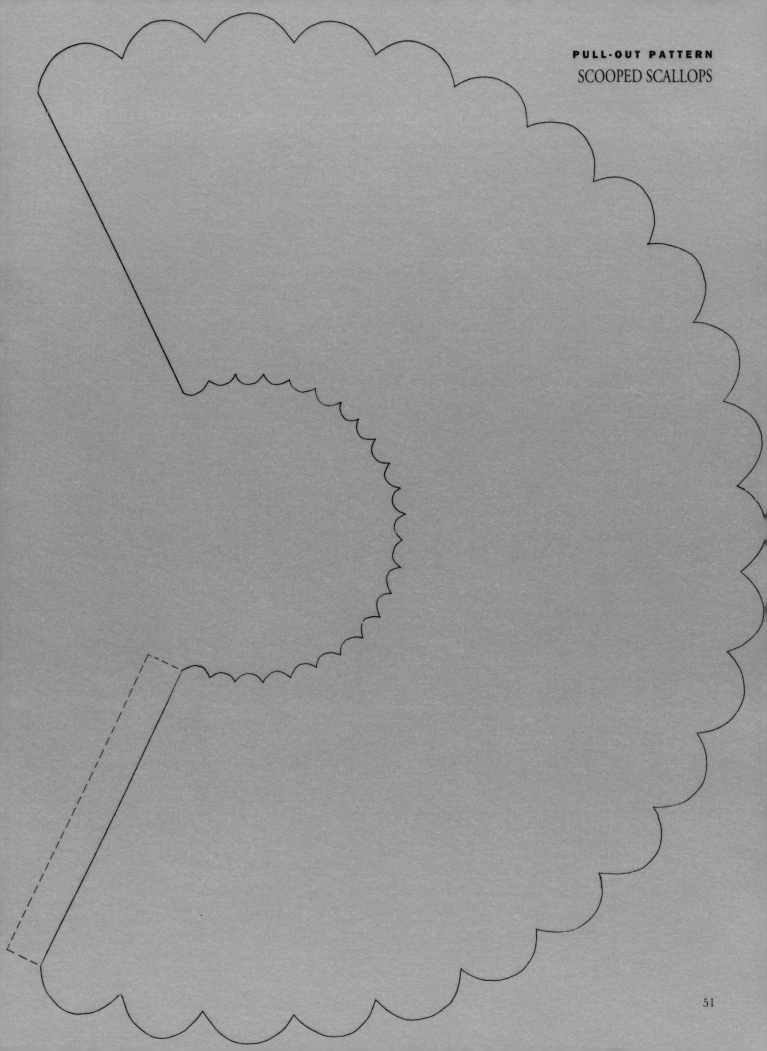

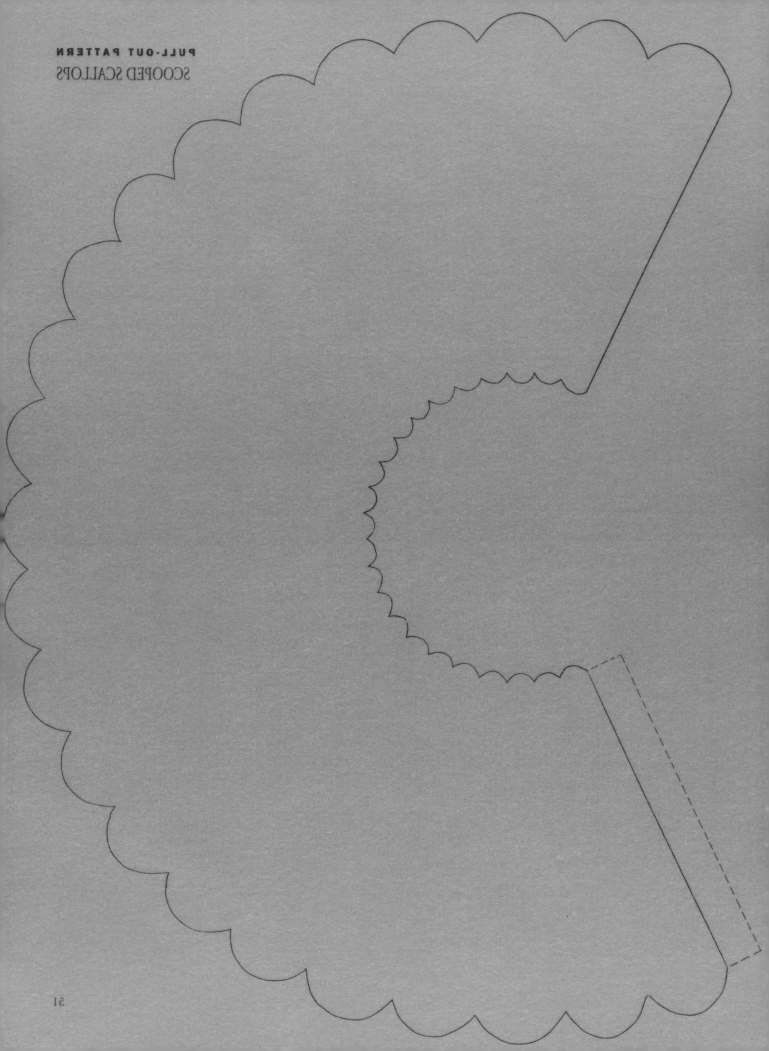

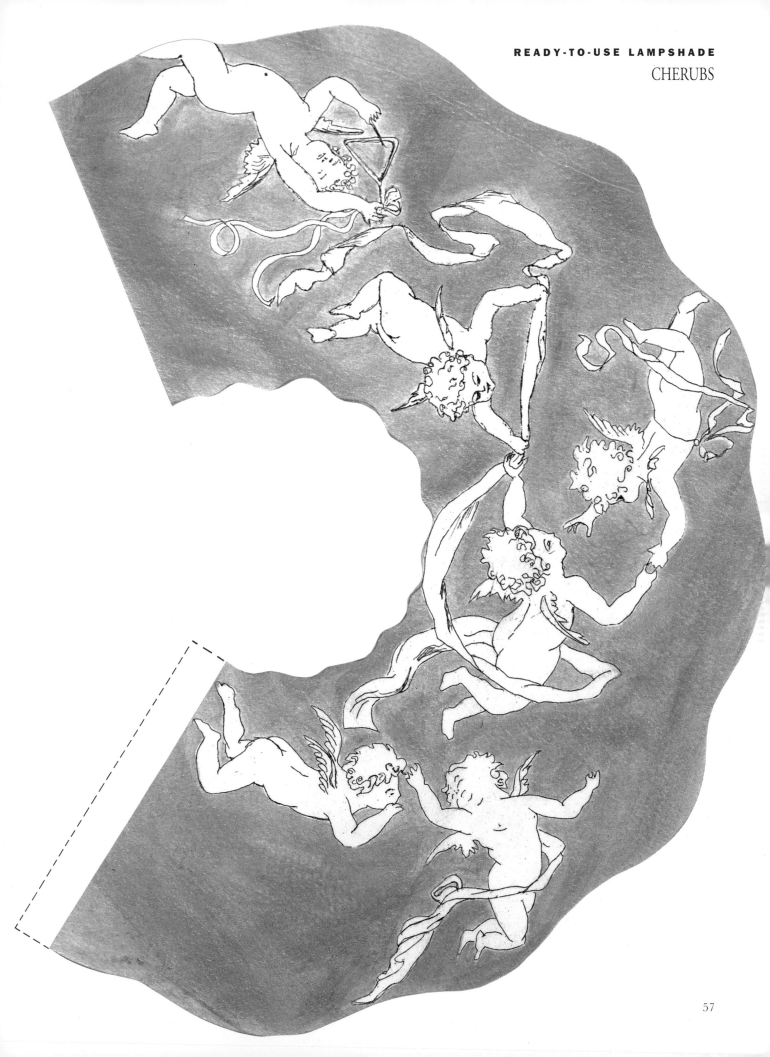

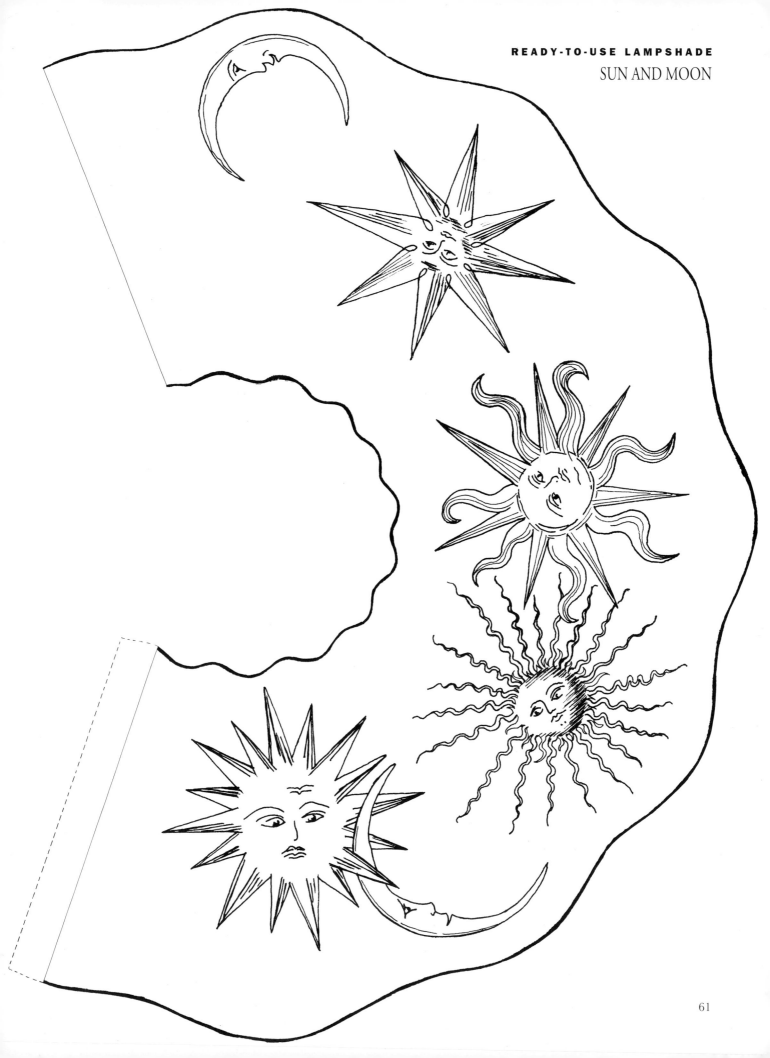

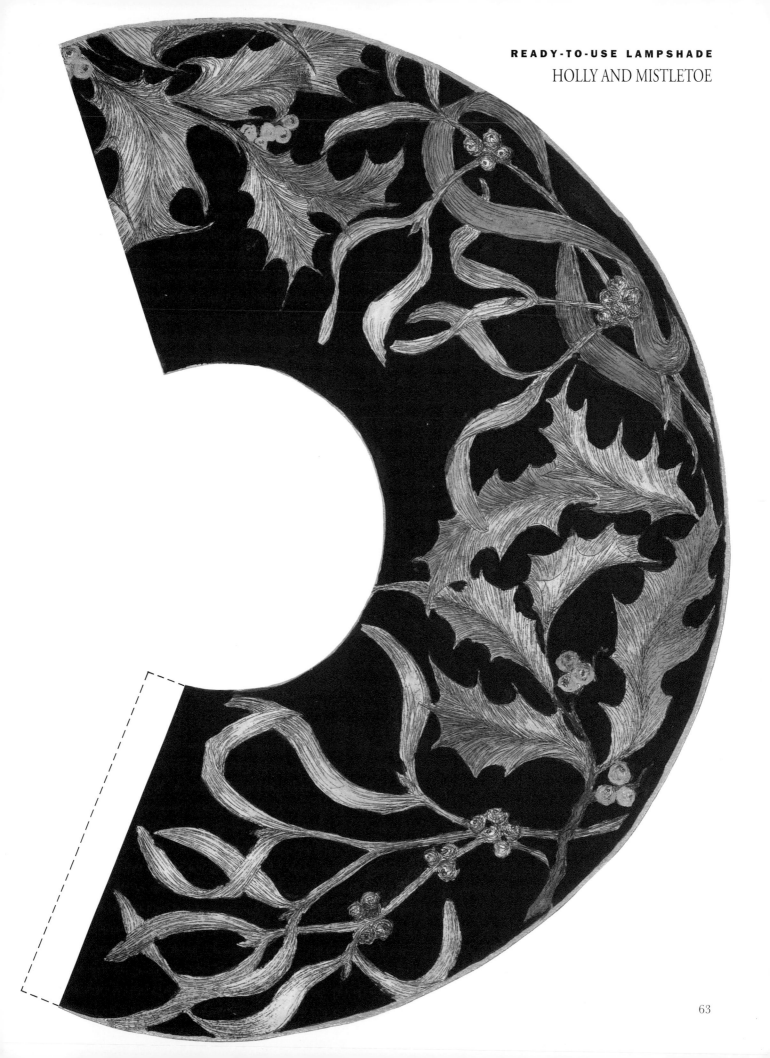

STENCILLING

Stencilling is an extremely versatile and adaptable technique which can be used to decorate any number of household objects and fabrics from floors to curtains. Depending how complicated your design is it can take some time to cut out the stencil but once cut you can use it again and again. For example you can use either of the patterns on pages 53 and 55 to make a stencilled shade and then use the same pattern to stencil a frieze on a wall or chair and to decorate a cushion or length of fabric.

FLOWER AND BUTTERFLY SHADE

The flower and butterfly pattern on page 53 makes a charming little shade and can be used in a number of different ways. You can stencil it directly on to the scalloped-edge shade as shown in the pattern or you can use it more creatively to make a trailing flower and butterfly edge to your shade (both methods are shown). You could also back the stencil itself with a translucent paper to create an unusual shade that would create the most wonderful shadows (see Trellis Shade page 68).

1 Either trace off the flower and butterfly stencil pattern on to some tracing paper or cut out the pattern from the book. Either way, transfer the tracing to the manilla paper using the method shown on page 18. If your traced outline is rather faint go over it again with a soft pencil.

2 Then, using a cutting knife and mat, cut out the flower, leaf and butterfly motifs by pulling the knife firmly along the traced outline. When cutting hold the manilla paper with one hand to keep it still and cut away from this hand in case your hand slips.

WHAT YOU WILL NEED

Flower and Butterfly pattern
(page 53)

Oiled manilla stencil paper, matt acetate or any non-porous paper (take-away pizza boxes are ideal)

Cutting mat and knife

Spray glue or masking tape

Acrylic hobby paints

Stencil brushes

Pencil case contents

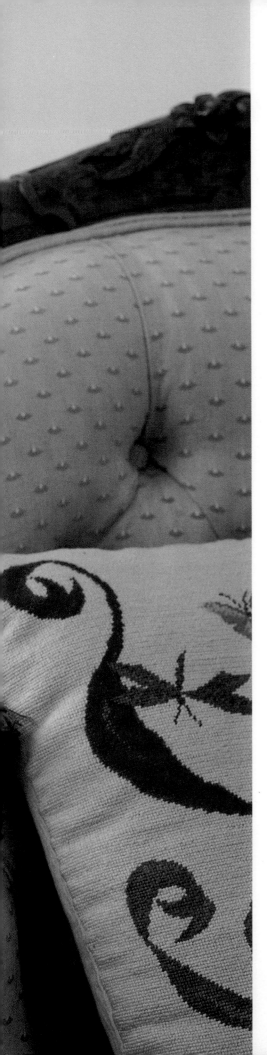

FLOWER AND BUTTERFLY SHADE

3 Transfer the outline edge of the flower and butterfly tracing to your background paper and mark in a couple of leaves so that you can align the stencil correctly. Attach the stencil to the flat lampshade outline either by spraying the back with glue or using a little masking tape to avoid any movement while you are working. Load your stencil brush with a small amount of paint. Dab the brush on a spare piece of paper to check it is not overloaded.

4 Gently apply the paint using a dabbing motion and gradually massage the paint into all the corners of the stencil. If you want to use more than one colour, change brushes as washing the brush may dilute the paint.

5 Remove the stencil and when dry spray with fixative for protection (see page 15). Cut out the shade and glue the ends together.

VARIATIONS

You can also use this stencil to create a wonderful trailing edge of flowers and butterflies. Lightly mark the outer edge of the shade. Then, using the pencil line as a guide, stencil around the edge using the parts of the stencil you wish, for example, I picked out a flower followed by some leaves, then a butterfly to trail around the edge. You will know where to place the stencil as you have the outline guide to follow and you will also be able to see the previous flower or leaf stencil next to it. If two motifs are very close to each other on the stencil and you only wish to use one, then cover one with masking tape.

THE
TRELLIS SHADE

The pattern for this trellis shade can be found on page 55.
I have used a variety of papers stencilling gold on to a background
of black, white and dark green but the choice is yours
so have a go. You could also back the stencil itself with a translucent
paper to create an unusual shade that would create the
most wonderful shadows.

WHAT YOU WILL NEED

Trellis pattern (page 55)

Oiled manilla stencil paper, matt
acetate or any non-porous paper
(take-away pizza boxes are ideal)

Cutting mat and knife

Spray glue or masking tape

Acrylic hobby paints

Stencil brushes

Pencil case contents

1 Cut out the stencil as shown on page 65, cutting from the centre outwards. You will have to be gentle as it does not have large background areas to give it strength unlike the flower and butterfly stencil.

2 Cut out the lampshade from the manilla paper and attach to your background paper using spray glue or masking tape.

3 Again using very little paint, dab the brush over the stencil. I used acrylic hobby paints because they are quick drying.

4 Lightly draw around the manilla stencil to give the outline of the shade. Cut out when dry and glue the edges together.

VARIATIONS

Use the stencil itself as a shade: it casts wonderful tracery shadows over the ceiling and is quite magical.

Instead of oiled manilla paper use a false wood wrapping paper to cut out the trellis pattern. Back this with a delicate, translucent trapped fibre paper. When lit this gives a gentle diffused light.

You can see here the different effects created using the same pattern as a stencil (top), as a cutout backed with translucent paper (below, left) and the cutout stencil used as a shade (below, right).

CUTTING AND PIERCING

By cutting and piercing a piece of paper you can create dramatic changes of texture across
its surface. Light catches the raised areas on an unlit shade forming interesting shadows and when lit the
light shines through the cuts to create a quite bewitching effect. It is astonishing what can
be achieved with a few simple cuts and pierces and how they can develop into sophisticated patterns.

PIERCED FLOWER AND BUTTERFLY SHADE

1 Trace out the stencil pattern from page 53. Lightly transfer the tracing on to the reverse of your chosen paper. I used a 290gsm (140lbs) Whatman watercolour paper measuring 30cm x 23cm (11¾in x 9in).

2 Cut around the outer edge of the shade as it is easier to work with once cut out. I have chosen to use the scalloped edge, but you could use either of the edges shown on pages 45 and 51. All you need to do is trace off the outer edge and superimpose it over your stencil and butterfly motifs.

3 Following your traced outline on the reverse of the shade, cut out the leaves from the tips almost back to the base but do not cut out completely. In the same way semi-cut the petals and butterflies. These partially cut motifs are your windows through which the light will shine when the shade is lit.

WHAT YOU WILL NEED

Flower and Butterfly pattern
(page 53)

Watercolour paper

Tracing paper

Pencil case contents

Cutting knife and mat

Hat pin or needle

4 Finally, for additional detail, I used a hat pin to create a pierced border edge. Pierce from the right side through to the back following the edge by eye to avoid making any marks. On each scallop peak, I pierced an additional hole to give added definition and movement. For the same reason I added a few extra pierced details to the leaves and butterflies.

ANIMAL SHADE

Traditionally food was stored in pierced tins to allow air to circulate but it was also used as a form of decoration and tins were embellished with farm animals, houses, flowers and hearts. In the same way I have decorated these shades with a number of tiny pierced holes to create the most exquisite patterns which look quite enchanting when lit. I used a plain white paper and a pretty flecked handmade paper for my shades but don't feel restricted by this choice – you can use anything.

1 To make the pierced holes you can use almost any sharp tool. A particularly quick and easy method is to use a sewing machine. Set it on a loose setting, remove the thread and change your nice new needle for an old blunt one (I mark my older needles with a touch of nail varnish). If you don't have a sewing machine then a hat pin or needle is equally effective. Work on to a cutting mat or wooden board if using this method.

2 I used the animals from the farmyard lamp on page 59 as my motifs for this shade. Trace over the animals and transfer the traced outline to your background paper using the method shown on page 18. Then cut around the outline edge of your shade.

3 Using a sewing machine or other pointed tool, follow your traced outline so that you are piercing from the back of the shade through to the front. For contrast, I pierced the two borders from the front through to the back.

4 Finish off by gluing the two edges together (see page 9).

WHAT YOU WILL NEED

Background papers

Tracing paper

Hat pin, sewing machine or large needle

Cutting mat or wooden board

VARIATIONS

Lightly pencil in a series of circular parallel lines around your flat lampshade shape and pierce along them using a sewing machine (see above). This method was also used to make the large shade covered with handmade paper pictured opposite. Alternatively, using the scalloped edge pattern from page 49, you can pierce the simplest of borders around the edges to enhance the natural movement and elegance of this design as can be seen from the photograph on page 71.

CUTTING WINDOWS

You can produce a surprising number of patterns and effects by taking a very basic lampshade outline such as the one on page 41 and cutting a series of windows in the surface (see below). When lit the outcome is always striking. You can open the windows outwards or inwards or vary the two effects on the same shade.

A simple variation on these window shades (see opposite) is to place coloured papers behind them or old Christmas stamps (I used duplicates from my daughter's collection) as I have done here. If you don't have any used stamps available then small specialized packs can be bought from larger newsagents.

When lit, the light filtering through evokes the delights of stained-glass windows or advent calendars. Many a friend has opened a window to have a closer peek.

WHAT YOU WILL NEED

Background paper

Cutting knife and mat

Ruler (preferably metal)

Stamps (optional)

Glue

Pencil case contents

1 Mark out the shape of the windows you wish to cut on the reverse of your shade. If you want to cut a triangular window then mark out the shape and cut through two of the sides using a ruler for accuracy. Then fold the paper outwards or inwards along the third edge. On thicker papers you will need to scour this third side gently so that it folds easily.

2 To create a cross, which is one of my favourites, mark out a number of squares on the back of the shade. Then, using a ruler, cut diagonally across the square to make four delightful little triangles. Gently scour the joining edges and fold outwards

3 To make the stamp shade, arrange your stamps on the back of your flat shade. I used the smaller ones around

the top and the larger ones below. When you are happy with the arrangement, trace around them lightly to mark the positions. Remove the stamps and draw a slightly smaller rectangle within this outline. Cut out the windows as before. The cross cut works particularly well.

4 Apply a little glue around the window edges on the back of the shade. Stick down the stamps so that the right sides are facing the cut windows. The white border around the stamps will be hidden because the window is slightly smaller than the actual stamp.

5 For a finishing touch, I added bands of gold around the top and bottom edges. It is easier to do this before gluing the edges together.

CHAPTER SIX

PUNCHING HOLES AND PLEATING

Before we begin, the techniques shown in this chapter may appear complicated on first
reading but are actually quite simple and have been attempted successfully by my ten-year-old daughter.
Simply follow the instructions and you will be amazed at the stunning shades you can create.

PUNCHED HOLE SHADES

I have used a range of plain pri-
mary coloured paper, readily
available from stationery shops, and
a single hole punch to create these
colourful shades. Thread ribbon,
raffia, twine or cord through the
holes for added pattern and cunning.
For the small shades photographed
on page 76, I used the Tartan
outline for a straight-edged shade
from page 41. I show how to make
the large yellow shade here.

1 To make a pattern for a larger
shade use the method shown on page
10. Cut around the pattern in the
paper of your choice (I chose a stiff
yellow paper [300gsm/160lb]). Neaten
up the outline using a compass. For a
shade like this you will need to use a
compass with an extension arm. Note
that I have drawn a line from the base
of the outline edge to the central
compass marking to form a fan shape.

2 To mark the positions of the hole
punches, place the central point of your
protractor over the central compass
marking and the 0 degree mark on the
outline edge that you have just drawn
in. Divide the shade into 5 degree
segments along the base of the outline
and 10 degree segments along the top.
Use a ruler to join the marks from the
central compass point to the base and
top of the shade outline.

WHAT YOU WILL NEED

Stiff paper

Compass with extension arm

Protractor

Ruler

Single hole punch

Ribbon, raffia, twine or cord of
your choice

Large needle

Pencil case contents

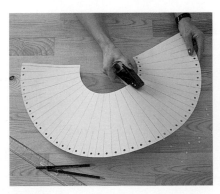

3 Align the side of your hole punch
against one of the ruled lines to ensure
the punched hole will be centred.

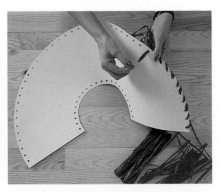

4 Thread your chosen raffia, ribbon,
twine or cord through the holes using
a large needle.

FOLDED PAPER SHADES

Folded paper is quite beautiful, although it requires patience and a lot of paper – three times
the amount for each little shade! But these little shades tied up with ribbons, cord or even string always
delight me and are well worth the effort. Many of the plain papers look most effective or if you
fancy something more colourful, try a striped paper as this exaggerates the zig-zag effect of the folding.

1 Kilt pleat Measure the depth of your lamp frame from
top to bottom to gauge the width of your rectangular strip.
Then measure around the base of your shade and triple it to
obtain the required length. If you wish to make a classic
little cone the size of paper required will be 9.5cm x 153cm
(3³/₄ in x 60 in). It is more manageable to cut two strips
measuring 9.5cm x 76.5cm (3³/₄in x 30in) as I have done here.
Divide the paper into 1cm (³/₈ in) columns by lightly
indicating the divisions with a small pencil mark. Then using
a hat pin or compass point pierce a hole through the pencil
markings to avoid having to mark both sides of the shade.
Use a ruler to make sure your point is accurately positioned. These are your fold marks. If you are making a larger
shade you may wish to increase the depth of the fold.

1 Flared pleat Measure the diameter of your shade at the
top and bottom using a ruler. Divide these figures in half to
calculate the radius measurements. Set your compass arms
so they are the smaller radius width apart and draw a circle.
Then set the compass arms at the larger radius width and
draw another larger circle around the first using the same
central compass mark. The radius measurements for the
small classic cone are 4.2cm (1⁵/₈ in) and 13.6cm (5³/₈ in).
Draw another pair of circles in the same way. Mark out 10
degree segments all the way round both circle edges using a
pencil to indicate the divisions (see page 77, step 2). Then,
using a hat pin, needle or compass point make a hole
through the pencil mark using a ruler for accuracy as before.
Join two of the points with a ruled line. Cut the circles out
of the paper including the inner rounds, and along the ruled
line to make the joining edges.

WHAT YOU WILL NEED

Chosen paper	Ruler
Compass	Needle or hat pin for piercing
Cutting mat and knife	Bone folder or ruler
Protractor	Needle

2 Using the pierced holes as your guidelines fold over the paper as carefully as you can. The flared fold (above right) actually gives a much fuller shade than the kilt pleat (above left).

3 Smooth each fold down with the bone folder or ruler. Turn the strip or round of paper over and fold the other side and so on until you have pleated all the paper.

4 Join your two strips or circles of folded paper together and then join the two ends to make a round. Hold together with paper clips and allow to dry.

5 Thread up a robust needle with your chosen thread and push it through each fold, about 1cm (³/₈ in) from the top of the shade. Then pull the thread to gather up the folds until it fits snugly around your lamp frame. I inserted another invisible thread about 5cm (2 in) down, just skimming the folds from behind so I had more control over the final shape of the shade, but it is not strictly necessary.

CHAPTER SEVEN

DÉCOUPAGE

Découpage is an extremely effective and quick way of creating a decorative finish by cutting out images and sticking them down on a surface of your choice. It is an extremely versatile technique and can be used to transform all sorts of household objects from small trinket boxes and jars to trays, chairs and even walls.

FLOWER AND MOTH SHADE

The charming lampshades shown here have been made using a background of stiff, plain white paper, decorated with a flower and moth motif. These pretty images came from some wrapping that I had bought from a museum shop.

Other good sources include photographs, wallpapers or magazines. You will also find suitable découpage images throughout this book, for example, I used the little cherubs on page 57 to make a series of découpage shades (see page 85).

WHAT YOU WILL NEED

2 sheets of thick white paper
(for two shades)

2 sheets of wrapping paper

Spray or PVA glue

Spray fixative

Cutting knife or nail scissors

Contents of pencil case

1 Transfer the outline of the lampshade shown on page 41 to your background paper. If you want to make a larger shade then make a pattern as shown on page 10. Go over the outline using a compass.

2 Cut out the motifs you wish to use. There were large and small flower and moth motifs on my wrapping paper: I chose the smaller ones to suit the scale of my lampshades. Make sure you cut out the images accurately as any mistakes will be exaggerated when the lamp is lit.

3 Arrange the cutouts on the surface of the paper and when you have found a pattern you like, glue them in position. If you are using spray glue, apply to the back of the motif only. Alternatively, dilute the PVA glue with just enough water to allow you to spread it. Be careful not to use too much as the surface will buckle.

4 Once the glue has dried, cut out the lampshade. I adore the uneven flowing edges created by cutting around the trailing flower motifs shown here. However, if you would prefer your lampshade to have straight edges then arrange the motifs so that they remain within the confines of the original outline. Finally, glue the edges together.

CHERUB SHADE

I photocopied the little cherubs from the lampshade on page 57 and used them as découpage motifs to make these charming shades. If you wanted to decorate a larger shade you could easily enlarge the motifs on the photocopier or decorate the shade with more of the little motifs.

I used a variety of silver backgrounds for my shades plus one made from a semi-translucent white paper, but they would look adorable on any ground, plain or patterned, so do experiment.

WHAT YOU WILL NEED

Suitable background papers

Spray or PVA glue

Cutting knife and mat or scissors

Pencil case contents

1 Trace off the outline of the shade from page 41 or if you wish to have a scalloped edge, the outline on page 49. Transfer this outline to your chosen background paper and cut out. I used a metallic silver background for one of the shades, a matt silver ground for another and a semi-translucent white paper for the third shade.

2 Photocopy the cherub motifs and cut them out carefully using a cutting knife or pair of scissors.

3 Take your shade outline and lay it out flat. Arrange the motifs until you find an arrangement that you like. For the metallic silver shade, I used three cherubs and arranged them so they looked as if they were holding hands, while on the matt shade I used just two. For the third, I reduced the size of the cherub motifs on a photocopying machine and placed them separately around the edge so they look as if they are floating around the scalloped edge of the shade.

4 Once you have decided upon the arrangement of your motifs glue them down one by one. If you try and glue too many at once, you will end up with cutouts and glue all over the place, as I did when I first attempted découpage.

5 Allow to dry and then glue the ends of the shade together and they are ready for use.

NOTE For added detail, I drew a black felt-tip line around the top and base of the translucent shade just to give it that added detail. Remember to do this before you glue the shade together.

SILHOUETTE SHADE

Silhouette portraiture was extremely popular during the eighteenth century. These shadow
portraits invariably depicted their subjects in profile and were executed in paper and mounted on a
contrasting background, usually black on white. Below you will find the outlines of the
silhouettes I used to decorate the charming shades opposite. They tell a story of a gentlemen who having
parted from a friend, is most gallant to a pretty lady cyclist, but is consequently chastised by his wife.

You could choose any subject to depict, however, from sports men and women, politicians or photographs of your children. To find images that are suitable for silhouettes, look only at the outline forms. If you really want the profile of a particular person and it eludes you, stand them in front of a projector, attach some paper to the wall and draw around the shadow of their profile. Children adore this and they make novel presents for unsuspecting grandparents.

1 Transfer the outline of your chosen silhouette to a piece of paper by tracing off or photocopying the image. Fill it in using black felt-tip. If you wish, you can trace over or photocopy the images below.

2 Cut out your lampshade shape from your chosen background paper using one of the traced patterns or make your own as shown on page 10.

3 Cut out your blackened silhouette motifs and arrange them on your background paper. When you have found an arrangement you like, glue them in position. I used a semi-opaque background paper for one of my lampshades and stuck the silhouettes on the reverse side of the shade so they show through rather like trompe l'oeil medallions.

VARIATIONS

You can choose any theme you wish for silhouettes: I thought these musical instrument motifs worked rather well on the translucent paper (see left). I have also made valentine silhouette lamps of the cherubs on red card. Silhouettes are elegant and intriguing to do, but be careful – you might not want to stop!

WHAT YOU WILL NEED

Suitable image(s) for a silhouette

Tracing paper or photocopier

Paper for making silhouettes
(if using tracing method)

Black felt-tip pen

Background paper (white or red)

CHAPTER EIGHT

NEEDLEWORK LAMPSHADES

The embroidered shades shown in this last section are less immediate than some of the simple paper shades but they are exquisite when stitched up and are well worth the extra effort required. Don't worry if you are not an experienced embroiderer as the stitches used are extremely simple ones to master. You can either attempt the Initial or Scroll Shades shown below and on page 90 which use satin stitch or, if you prefer needlepoint and cross stitch, the Rosebud Shades on page 92.

INITIAL SHADE

This charming shade makes a lovely personalized gift for a friend. Choose a style for the initials by looking through magazines, newspapers or a specialist book on typography. Alternatively, draw your own, as I did, and play around until you find an arrangement that you like.

1 Trace over your chosen letters on to separate pieces of tracing paper and then superimpose them on top of each other until you find an arrangement you like. I added movement by letting the top curve of the S roll over the G and integrated the cross of the T with part of the G. Transfer the initials in your chosen position on to a tracing paper outline of your shade. I added some polka dots at this stage to give texture to the finished embroidery.

2 Transfer the outline of the shade to your fabric using the method shown on page 18 and tack around the outline for guidance. Then transfer the initials on to the fabric by placing a piece of carbon paper between the tracing paper pattern and the fabric and going over the outline lightly. Take care as it is difficult to remove unwanted carbon marks. You may find it helpful to secure the tracing and carbon paper to the fabric with masking tape.

WHAT YOU WILL NEED

36-count DMC Edinburgh linen in cream measuring 36cm x 24cm (14in x 9½in)

Tracing paper

Dressmaker's carbon

Medium weight iron-on interfacing (same size as the linen)

One skein of 6 stranded white cotton, I used Ecru

Embroidery scissors, needle, tacking thread and pins

Embroidery hoop if you use one

I worked three strands of Ecru embroidery thread in satin stitch on a 36-count Edinburgh linen. If you are unfamiliar with satin stitch, let the slope of your stitching follow the movement of the letter. Your stitches cannot all be horizontal or vertical. Care must be taken to keep a good even edge and not to make the stitches too long as they will be pulled out of position.

3 Work your design accurately and be especially careful not to let any thread, however small, trail from one letter to the next as it will show when lit. You will also have to cast off your threads neatly. I am not normally very careful about the back of my work, but this is one of the occasions when I do take care as everything will show.

Trim the shade to within 1cm (³⁄₈in) of the tacked outline. Fold back the hem and tack around the edge.

4 To back the finished embroidery with interfacing, set the iron on a medium setting. Place a piece of tissue paper on the ironing board or work surface and then the worked shade right-side down on top of this. Finally place the interfacing shiny/sticky side down on top of the reverse side of the embroidered shade. Iron over the interfacing for about three minutes (or whatever is indicated on the packaging). When ready the shade should be stiff. If it isn't then try ironing for a little longer.

5 Cut around the outline edge of your shade which will be sandwiched between the tissue paper and interfacing and remove the tacking from around the hem. I promise you this is the easiest way of achieving a perfect fit of shade to interfacing

6 Stitch the ends together using a blind hemming stitch as glue will discolour the fabric.

SCROLL SHADE

This abstract design is perfect for working in satin stitch
and looks particularly good worked in a white thread on a dark
background. It is quite quick to work and works well on a
larger shade. If you wish to create your own design then play around
with some abstract patterns until you find one that you like.
Alternatively, the Classic pattern on page 37 would look lovely
worked in satin stitch.

I used a 32-count Belfast linen and
three skeins of white embroidery
thread to make this shade. Obviously
the amounts will vary according to
the size and shape of your shade
but the quantities given below were
for my shade which had a circumference around the top of 15cm (6in)
and a base measurement of 51cm
(20in), with a drop of 31cm (12in).

WHAT YOU WILL NEED

Tracing paper

32-count Belfast linen

Dressmaker's carbon

White embroidery thread
(approximately 4 skeins)

Embroidery scissors, tacking thread,
needle and pins

Embroidery hoop, if you use one

Plastic backing for lining the
finished shade

1 Design your own abstract pattern or
trace off the Classic design on page 37.
Once you have your tracing paper
pattern attach it to the linen with
masking tape and tack around the
outline edge.

2 Transfer your abstract design using
the carbon paper method (see page 88,
step 2).

3 Work the design in satin stitch
taking care not to pull the threads too
tight in case the linen puckers.

4 Once the embroidery is finished, cut
around the tacked outline leaving a
1cm ($^3/_8$ in) trim. Fold back the hem
and tack into position. Back with
plastic sheeting as shown on page 13.
This method is particularly good for
covering larger shades. You can, if you
wish, line the shade with interfacing by
following the instructions for the Initial
Shade (see page 89).

5 Remove the tacking stitches and
stitch the ends together with blind
hemming. Glue the shade to the frame
as shown on page 13.

The neutral tones of these two shades work particularly well together.
Both designs were worked in white but for the scroll shade (left), I used a dark
background and for the initial shade a cream one.

CROSS-STITCH ROSEBUD SHADE

I adore to embroider and this trailing rosebud pattern is so versatile and can be used in many different settings by varying the colours. You could also consider embroidering this motif on to clothes – a detail would look particularly charming on the pocket of a little girl's smock dress.

WHAT YOU WILL NEED

18-count damask Aida in antique white measuring 36cm x 24cm (14¼ in x 9½ in)

Stranded cotton (see below right for colourways and quantities)

Medium weight iron-on interfacing

Embroidery scissors, needle, tacking thread and pins

Embroidery hoop if you use one

1 Follow the chart opposite and work the rosebud in half cross stitch using two strands of cotton over one block of the Aida fabric. Take care that you do not leave any loose ends as these will show when the lamp is lit and remember to keep your stitches as relaxed as possible otherwise you will distort the shape of the shade.

2 Cut around the outline of the shade leaving a 1cm (³⁄₈ in) trim. Tack back the hem and interface the shade as shown on page 89. If you are using a larger shade then follow the instructions for the Scroll Shade on page 90.

3 Sew the ends together with blind hemming.

NEEDLEPOINT ROSEBUD SHADE

You can work the rosebud shade in needlepoint as well as cross-stitch. I used an 18-gauge interlocking canvas which gives a good stiff finish.

WHAT YOU WILL NEED

18-gauge mono canvas measuring 36cm x 24cm (14¼ in x 9½ in)

Pearl cotton (see right for colourways and quantities)

Medium weight iron-on interfacing

Embroidery scissors, needle, tacking thread and pins

Embroidery hoop if you use one

Follow the instructions for the cross-stitch shade above.

VARIATIONS

If you have any damaged embroideries you could always give them a new lease of life by turning them into lampshades using this straightforward method.

If you have any chintz leftovers from curtains, why not interface them and make a co-ordinating lampshade? Do hold any fabric up to the light before making a shade so that you can see what the end result will look like.

You will require one skein of each of the following colours for both the cross-stitch and needlepoint shade.

Stranded and Pearl cotton (DMC)

dark green	500
mid green	501
light green	991
dark red	902
mid red	816
light red	666
mid brown	400
light brown	301

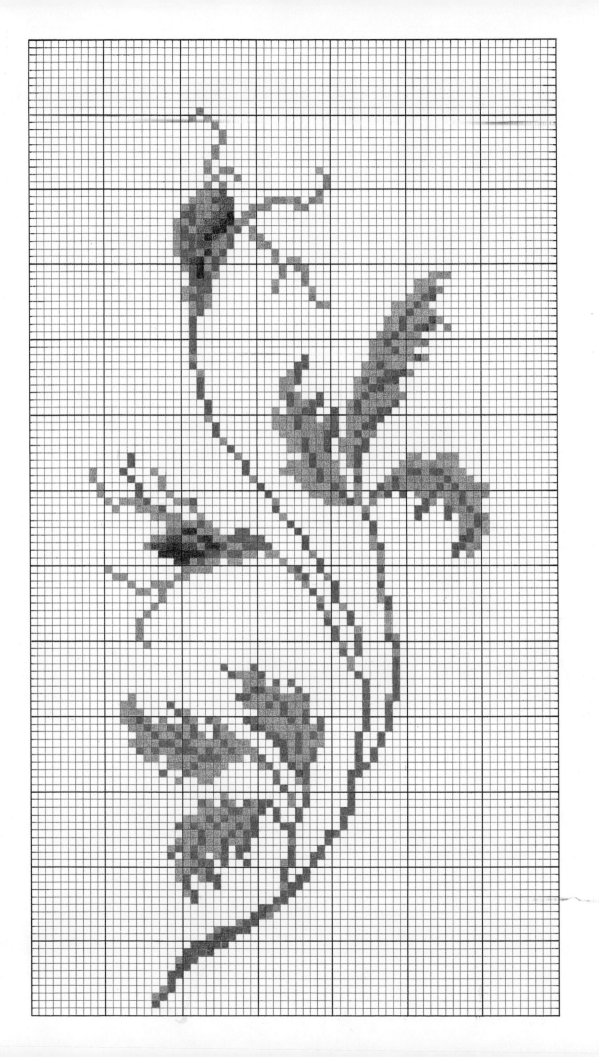

The needlepoint and cross-stitch rosebud shades look charming as a pair: their rich colours echoing those of the flower arrangement and the fire.

ACKNOWLEDGEMENTS

The author would like to thank the following for supplying
materials for photography:

Christopher Wray Lighting Emporium for lamps, bases,
fittings and fixtures; Daler-Rowney Limited for papers and paints;
DMC Creative World for embroidery threads and linens;
M and F Lampshades for frames, backing plastic and parchment;
Price's Patent Candle Company for candles;
and VV Rouleaux for their trimmings.

The author also wishes to thank the following for their contributions:

Chelsea Textiles, 39 Thurloe Square, London SW7
(Tel: 071 584 1165) for the loan of the most ravishing crewel work,
needlepoint and other exquisitely designed textiles;
Manuel Canovas, 2 North Terrace, Brompton Road,
London SW3 2BA (Tel: 071 225 2298) for the most beautifully
designed fabrics; Sylvia Napier Antiques, 554 Kings Road,
London SW6 2DZ (Tel: 071 371 5881) for the loan of furniture,
lamps and various objets d'art; and National Gallery
Publications, London, for permission to use their Brussel gift wrap,
featured in the découpage lampshades on pages 82-3.

Swooping in on people, with all the inconvenience
involved and none of the remuneration, does rather try people's
patience, but all these contributors could not have been
more helpful and I know you will be as content with their
products as I have been.